Reading STREET

Grade K

Scott Foresman
Practice Book 6
Unit 6

PEARSON
Scott Foresman

Editorial Offices: Glenview, Illinois • Parsippany, New Jersey • New York, New York
Sales Offices: Needham, Massachusetts • Duluth, Georgia • Glenview, Illinois
Coppell, Texas • Sacramento, California • Mesa, Arizona

Contents

Unit 6
Building Our Homes

	Family Times	Phonics	High-Frequency Words	Phonics Story	Comprehension	Grammar
Homes Around the World	1–2	3, 8	4	5–6	7, 9	10
Old MacDonald had a Woodshop	11–12	13, 18	14	15–16	17, 19	20
Building Beavers	21–22	23, 28	24	25–26	27, 29	30
The Night Worker	31–32	33, 38	34	35–36	37, 39	40
The House That Tony Lives In	41–42	43, 48	44	45–46	47, 49	50
Animal Homes	51–52	53, 58	54	55–56	57, 59	60

© Pearson Education K

Help Sam find his way home by following the path of /a/ pictures.

Family Times

You are your child's first teacher!

This week we're ...

Reading *Homes Around the World*

Talking About Homes Around the World

Learning About Phonics Review
Compare and Contrast

4

1

Here are ways to help your child practice skills while having fun!

Day 1 **Read Together**

Describe an item in the house with an /a/ or an /i/. Have your child guess the item. For example, say, *I am thinking of a paper that shows the roads and cities.* The answer is a *map*. Take turns giving clues and guessing the objects.

Day 2 **Read Together**

Have your child read the Phonics Story *Vin and the Bag*. Find /a/ and /i/ words.

Day 3 **Short Vowels**

Read the following words to your child. Have your child tell you whether the word has an /a/ or an /i/.

bat   pit   Jim   man

Day 4 **Words That Describe Action**

Ask your child to name some verbs. Tell your child that the letter *s* needs to be added when the verb is used with some words: *He runs. Bob walks. She skips.* Have your child give some sentences with action words that need *s*.

Day 5 **Practice Handwriting**

Have your child write the following /a/ and /i/ words.

sat   sit   fan   fin

2

Words to talk about

home	roof	tools
apartment	city	country

Words to read

where	come	what
little	from	that
jam	van	mix
quit	hill	bag

3

Name _____

  Write   Color

m t

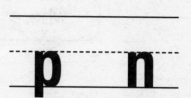
p n

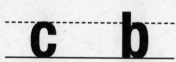
c b

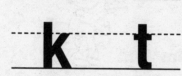
k t
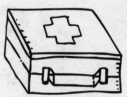

Aa
Ii

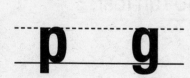
p g

j m

 Directions: Name each picture. Write *a* or *i* to finish each word. Color the /a/ pictures.

 **School + Home** **Home Activity:** Have your child write *tin* and *tan* and color a picture for each word.

Practice Book Unit 6

Phonics Review **3**

© Pearson Education K

Name _____

 Write  Color

| where | with | they | like |

_____

_ _ _ _ _ _ _ _ _ _ _ _ _ _ _ _ _ _ _ _

_____ play with a ball.

_____

_ _ _ _ _ _ _ _ _ _ _ _ _ _ _ _ _ _ _ _

_____ do you live?

_____

_ _ _ _ _ _ _ _ _ _ _ _ _ _ _ _ _ _ _ _

I will go _____ you.

_____

_ _ _ _ _ _ _ _ _ _ _ _ _ _ _ _ _ _ _ _

I _____ to run fast.

Directions: Write the missing word to finish each sentence. Color the pictures.

 Home Activity: Have your child use the high-frequency words in other sentences.

Vin will zip the bag.

He and the bag will go on a trip.

Name _____

Vin and the Bag

Vin had a bag.

The bag is a big bag.

He got one big can.

He got one little net.

He got one little kit.

He got one big rag.

Name _____

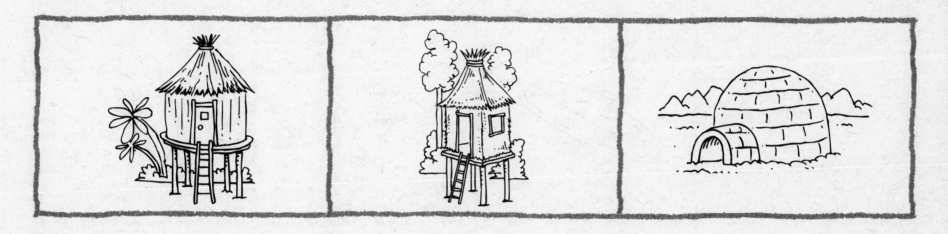 Color

 Directions: Color the picture that is different.

 School + Home   **Home Activity:** Have children tell how the pictures are alike and how they are different.

© Pearson Education K

Name _____

 Circle 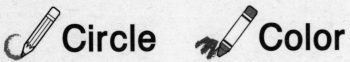 **Color**

lid lad		pin pan	
fan fin		crib crab	

 Directions: Circle the word that names the picture.
Color the /i/ pictures.

 Home Activity: Have your child draw a picture of
something with /i/.

8 **Phonics** Review

Practice Book Unit 6

Name _____

 Color

 Home Activity: Have your child tell how the pictures are alike and how they are different.

Directions: Color the pictures that are alike.

Practice Book Unit 6

Comprehension Compare and Contrast **9**

Name _____

 Circle  **Write**

sit

sits

_____

- - - - - - - - - - - - - - -

The dog _____.

hop

hops

_____

- - - - - - - - - - - - - - -

The frog _____.

mop

mops

_____

- - - - - - - - - - - - - - -

I _____.

pet

pets

_____

- - - - - - - - - - - - - - -

She _____ the cat.

hit

hits

_____

- - - - - - - - - - - - - - -

I _____ it.

cut

cuts

_____

- - - - - - - - - - - - - - -

He _____ the bun.

 Directions: Circle the correct word to finish the sentence. Write the word on the line.

 School + Home **Home Activity:** Have children read each sentence.

© Pearson Education K

Color the /o/ pictures. Draw lines to the matching rhyming words.

4

Family Times

You are your child's first teacher!

This week we're ...

Reading   *Old MacDonald had a Woodshop*

Talking About   Building Things

Learning About   Phonics Review
Character

1

Here are ways to help your child practice skills while having fun!

Day 1 **Read Together**

Write _op on a sheet of paper. Ask your child to make words by adding a letter to -op. After many words are written, have your child say or write sentences using several of the rhyming words.

Day 2 **Read Together**

Have your child read the Phonics Story *Spin the Top*. Find /o/ words.

Day 3 **Short Vowels**

Tell your child that the first and last letters of these words are the same. Have him or her figure out the words.

_o_ (mom)   _o_ (pop)   _o_ (Bob)

Day 4 **Adjectives**

Have your child choose a story character in a book. Ask your child to talk about the character using words such as *brave girl, funny monkey,* or *fuzzy bunny*. Tell your child that he or she is using describing words.

Day 5 **Practice Handwriting**

Have your child get his or her favorite movie or book. Ask your child to copy down the title on a sheet of paper.

2

Words to talk about

| saw | drill | hammer |
| screwdriver | file | chisel |

Words to read

yellow	five	with
go	look	he
pot	mom	stop
top	box	rock

3

Name _____

 Write  Color

_____
l _ **g**
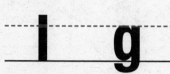

_____
m _ **p**

Aa

_____
t _ **p**

Ii

_____
s _ **ck**

Oo

_____
h _ **ll**

_____
p _ **t**

 Directions: Write *a*, *i*, or *o* to finish each word. Color the /o/ pictures.

School + Home **Home Activity:** Have your child write *lock* and *rock* and draw a picture for each word.

© Pearson Education K

Name _____

 Write  Color

| what | said | was | come |

_____

- - - - - - - - - - - - - - - - - -

I will _____ with you.

_____

- - - - - - - - - - - - - - - - - -

_____ can I do to help?

_____

- - - - - - - - - - - - - - - - - -

I _____ I will run fast.

_____

- - - - - - - - - - - - - - - - - -

I _____ the best one for the job.

Directions: Write the missing word to finish each sentence. Color the pictures.

 Home Activity: Have your child use *what* and *was* in other sentences.

14 **High-Frequency Words**

Practice Book Unit 6

Dad will spin the top.

Dad can spin it.

Dad can get the top to spin.

4

Phonics Story *Spin the Top*
Target Skill Review

Spin the Top

Bob got a top.

Bob will spin the top.

I

The top will not spin.

The top will not go.

Help! Help!

Help me spin the top.

It will not spin.

Help! Help!

2

Name _____

 Color  Draw

 Directions: Color the pictures. Then draw a picture that tells the character in the story in the last box.

 Home Activity: Have your child draw a picture of the characters in one of his or her favorite stories.

© Pearson Education K

Name _____

 Circle    Color

top tap		hot hat	
lock lick		cob cab	

 Directions: Circle the word that names the picture.
Color the /o/ pictures.

School + Home **Home Activity:** Have your child draw a picture of
something with /o/.

18 **Phonics** Review

Practice Book Unit 6

Name _____

✎ **Draw**   ✎ **Write**

© Pearson Education K

_____
- - - - - - - - - - - - - - -
_____
- - - - - - - - - - - - - - -
_____
- - - - - - - - - - - - - - -
_____
- - - - - - - - - - - - - - -
_____
- - - - - - - - - - - - - - -
_____

Directions: Draw your favorite character from *Old MacDonald had a Woodshop*, and then write or dictate words describing it.

School + Home **Home Activity:** Talk about the favorite character your child drew and have your child describe it.

Name _____

 Circle **Write**

 top

big

_____

The _____ dog is here.

 little

big

_____

The _____ cat ran.

 hat

fat

_____

One _____ hen is here.

 sad

bad

_____

The _____ dog got it.

 wet

get

_____

The _____ pet is mad.

one

two

_____

_____ cat ran to the man.

Directions: Circle the adjective that matches the picture. Write the word to complete the sentence.

School + Home

Home Activity: Have your child read each sentence.

20 **Grammar** Adjectives

Practice Book Unit 6

Color the /e/ pictures. Draw lines to match the rhyming words.

Family Times

You are your child's first teacher!

This week we're ...

Reading *Building Beavers*

Talking About Animals Build

Learning About Phonics Review
Main Idea

Here are ways to help your child practice skills while having fun!

Day 1 — **Read Together**

Have your child draw a picture of the word that rhymes with *fell* and begins with the letter *b.* Continue with *jet* and the letter *n,* and *peg* and the letter *l.*

Day 2 — **Read Together**

Have your child read the Phonics Story *Jim and Kim.* Find words that have /e/.

Day 3 — **Short Vowels**

Make a chart with /a/, /e/, /i/, and /o/. Have your child choose a book. Read through the story together. Write the words with /a/, /e/, /i/, and /o/ on the chart. Read the lists with your child.

Day 4 — **Sentences**

Have your child use sentences to tell about his or her favorite game. Give these examples: *My favorite game is soccer. I play it at the park. I play with my friends.* Have your child use complete sentences to tell about his or her favorite game or toy.

Day 5 — **Practice Handwriting**

Have your child copy the following sentence.

I can write and spell.

Words to talk about

beaver	lodge	paddle
stream	river	lake

Words to read

blue	she	three
are	do	here
pen	let	bell
get	fed	yes

Name _____

 Write  Color

w b

l g

p n

h t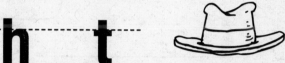

m n

j t

Aa
Ee
Ii

 Directions: Write *a*, *i*, or *e* to finish each word. Color the /e/ pictures.

 Home Activity: Have your child write *hen* and *pen* and draw a picture for each word.

Name _____

 Write  Color

from	go	her	five

_____

This is _____ big pet.

I see _____ pets.

The box is_____ him.

I can _____ with you.

Directions: Write the missing word to finish each sentence. Color the pictures.

 School + Home **Home Activity:** Use *five* and *from* in other sentences.

The hen had little ones.

Jim and Kim have lots of little hens.

Phonics Story *Jim and Kim*
Target Skill Review

Jim and Kim

Jim and Kim had a pet.

They had a pet hen.

The hen was in a pen.

Jim had fun with the pet
hen.

Jim fed the hen.

Kim had fun with the pet
hen.

Kim got a nest for the hen.

Name _____

 Circle

pets

tools

homes

 Directions: Circle the word that tells what the pictures are all about.

 Home Activity: Have children tell about each picture.

Practice Book Unit 6

Comprehension Main Idea **27**

Name _____

 Circle 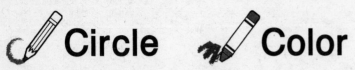 Color

net not		bad bed	(bed picture)
tan ten	10	pot pet	(pot picture)

 Directions: Circle the word that names the picture.
Color the /e/ pictures.

 Home Activity: Have your child draw a picture of
something with /e/.

© Pearson Education K

Name _____

 Circle  Color

pets

animals

plants

animals

 Directions: Circle the word that tells what each picture is all about. Color the pictures.

Home Activity: Have your child tell what the pictures are all about.

Practice Book Unit 6

© Pearson Education K

Name _____

 Write  Color

is   big   flag   the

_____

- -

_____

a   has   pet   he

_____

- -

_____

on   sits   she   a   box

_____

- -

_____

run   fast   can   I

_____

- -

_____

 Directions: Use the words in each box to write a telling sentence about the picture. Remember to use an uppercase letter and a period. Color the pictures.

 Home Activity: Have children read each sentence.

© Pearson Education K

Color the boxes with /u/ pictures. What letter do you see?

Family Times

You are your child's first teacher!

This week we're ...

Reading   *The Night Worker*

The Night Worker
Kate Banks   Pictures by Georg Hallensleben

Talking About   Building at Night

Learning About   Phonics Review
Plot

4

1

Here are ways to help your child practice skills while having fun!

Day 1 — Read Together

Tell your child to jump every time you say an /u/ word. Read the following sentences to your child.

The bug runs with the duck.
The cub hunts with the pup.

Day 2 — Read Together

Have your child read the Phonics Story *Gus and the Bug*. Find /u/ words.

Day 3 — Short Vowels

Have your child look around the house and find items that have /u/. Ask him or her to use the name of each item in a sentence.

Day 4 — Questions

Remind your child that sentences can tell something or ask something. Review what a question is with these examples: *What time is dinner? Can I play a game?* Take turns asking and answering questions with your child.

Day 5 — Practice Handwriting

Write *What is your name?* on a sheet of paper. Have your child respond to the question by writing the question and then writing the answer in the form of a sentence.

Words to talk about

engineer   construction   foreman

hard hat   beacons

street sweeper

Words to read

two	we	they
have	see	of
nut	fun	cup
cut	mug	bus

Name _____

 Write    Color

s **n**

Aa

b **t**

c **p**

Oo

p **p**

b **s**

Uu

c **t**

 Directions: Write *a*, *o*, or *u* to finish each word. Color the /u/ pictures.

 **Home Activity:** Have your child write *hut* and *nut* and draw a picture for each word.

© Pearson Education K

Name _____

 Write  Color

| are | that | yellow | do |

_____

Did you see _____?

_____

_____ you like to jump?

_____

The sun is _____.

_____

Where _____ you?

Directions: Write the missing word to finish each sentence. Color the pictures.

School + Home **Home Activity:** Have your child use the high-frequency words in other sentences.

© Pearson Education K

Gus grabs the bug.

Gus lets the bug go.

4

Phonics Story *Gus and the Bug*
Target Skill Review

Gus and the Bug

Gus will hug his mom.

Gus gets on the bus.

1

Gus sat with his pal Wes.

The sun was hot.

2

A bug got on the bus.

It sat with Gus and Wes.

3

Name _____

 Color

 Directions: Color the picture that shows what would happen next in each story.

 Home Activity: Have your child tell you the story of *The Night Worker*.

Name _____

 Circle  **Color**

net nut		cut cat	
cub cob		rug rag	

Directions: Circle the word that names the picture.
Color the /u/ pictures.

Home Activity: Have your child draw a picture of something with /u/.

Name _____

 Draw

Directions: Draw a picture to show what would happen next in each story.

 School + Home **Home Activity:** Ask your child to recall what happened after school today, telling the events in order.

 **Draw**

Where is the cat?

The bug ran to see me.

Do you see the dog?

I can not see you.

What did the bug do?

The cat is here.

Can you see me?

I can see the dog.

 Directions: Draw a line from each question to its answer.

 Home Activity: Ask your child the questions and have him or her create an answer using a complete sentence.

© Pearson Education K

Write the letter for the vowel sound in each picture name.

_____   _____

_____   _____

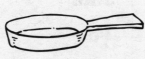

_____   _____

_____   _____

© Pearson Education K

4

Family Times

You are your child's first teacher!

This week we're ...

Reading   *The House That Tony Lives In*

By Anthony Lorenz   Illustrated by John Sandford

Talking About   Building a Home

Learning About   Phonics Review
                          Setting

1

Here are ways to help your child practice skills while having fun!

Day 1

Read Together

Show your child a picture. Ask your child to tell about the picture. When your child uses short vowel words, ask him or her to identify the vowel sound: /a/, /e/, /i/, /o/, or /u/.

Day 2

Read Together

Have your child read the Phonics Story *What Pets Do.* Point to various words and have your child say the word and identify the vowel sound.

Day 3

Short Vowels

Write the following word parts on a sheet of paper. Have your child write consonants and vowels to make new words.

_ _ n   _ e _   p _ t

Day 4

Exclamations

Write an exclamation mark on a sheet of paper and show it to your child. Tell your child that to show excitement, an exclamation mark is used. Give some examples such as *Wow! Bam!* and *Watch out!* Ask your child to give other examples.

Day 5

Practice Handwriting

Have your child write these sentences to practice using the exclamation mark.

Oh!   Wow!   Look at that!   Stop it!

Words to talk about

architect	electricians	plumbers
painters	landscapers	movers

Words to read

four	green	me
you	for	is
sat	had	hug
get	hid	box

Name _____

 Circle  **Color**

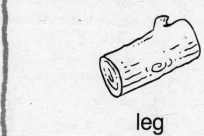 leg log	 pen pin	pep pup
 bag beg	 led lid	 tub tab

 Directions: Circle the word that names the picture. Color the pictures.

 Home Activity: Have your child use the words in sentences.

Practice Book Unit 6

Phonics Review **43**

© Pearson Education K

Name _____

 Write  Color

| blue | see | little | four |

_____

- -

Do I still look _____ ?

_____

- -

The bed is _____ .

_____

- -

I can _____ you.

_____

- -

My dog is _____ .

Directions: Write the missing word to finish each sentence. Color the pictures.

School + Home **Home Activity:** Have your child use the high-frequency words in other sentences.

© Pearson Education K

Sam is a cat.

Sam will sit in a lap.

He will nap.

4

What Pets Do

Peg is a dog.

She will tug.

She will dig.

1

Hal is a pet pig.

He will run in his pen.

He will go in the mud.

Tad is a pet frog.

He will hop.

He will swim.

Name _____

 Color

MOVING VAN

Directions: Color the picture that shows the setting of the story *The House That Tony Lives In*.

 Home Activity: Have your child tell you when and where the story takes place.

© Pearson Education K

Name _____

  **Write** **Color**

an

cr   b

m   n

d   sk

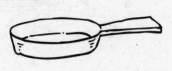

an

ca

 Directions: Write the missing letter in each word. Color pictures that rhyme.

 Home Activity: Have your child use the picture names in sentences.

48 **Phonics** Review

Practice Book Unit 6

© Pearson Education K

Name _____

 Color

Directions: Color the picture that shows the setting for a story about the people helping to build a barn.

 Home Activity: Have your child tell where and when the story takes place.

Practice Book Unit 6

Comprehension Setting **49**

Name _____

 # Circle

Can I swim?

Yes I can!

She has a big dog!

Pet the dog.

The pig is big.

I am glad!

Is he sad?

Help me!

🍎 **Directions:** Circle the exclamation mark in each pair
of sentences.

 Home Activity: Have your child read each sentence.

50 **Grammar** Exclamations

Practice Book Unit 6

Name the pictures. Draw lines to the vowel sound.

/a/

/e/

/i/

/o/

/u/

© Pearson Education K

Family Times

You are your child's first teacher!

This week we're ...

Reading   *Animal Homes*

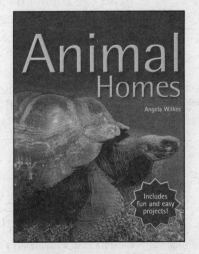

Includes fun and easy projects!

Talking About   Building Animal Homes

Learning About   Phonics Review
Draw Conclusions

4

1

Here are ways to help your child practice skills while having fun!

Day 1 — **Read Together**

Have your child choose a book. Read through the story together and point out words with short vowel sounds.

Day 2 — **Read Together**

Have your child read the Phonics Story *What Can You Do?* After reading, make a list of words with /a/, /e/, /i/, /o/, and /u/.

Day 3 — **Short Vowels**

Write the rhyme *fox in a box* on a sheet of paper. Read the rhyme together and have your child identify the rhyming words. Help your child make other rhymes such as *cat in the hat, hen in a pen,* or *bug on a rug.*

Day 4 — **Complete Sentences**

Tell your child the difference between giving short answers and using complete sentences. Explain that a complete sentence has a *naming part* and an *action part.* Have your child tell about school today using complete sentences.

Day 5 — **Practice Handwriting**

Have your child answer the question using a complete sentence. Help him or her write the answer.

Question: What game do you like best?

Answer: I like . . .

2

Words to talk about

predators	prey	shelter
shields	colony	bark

Words to read

my	where	come
what	said	was
top	bed	lap
hit	pan	cub

3

Name _____

✎ Draw

pin 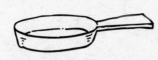   cub    hut

pen   cab    hat

pan    cob    hit

 Directions: Draw lines to match the words with the pictures.

 Home Activity: Have your child draw pictures for these words: *cat, cot, cut*.

Name _____

 Write  Color

| three | of | look | you |

_____

_____ at that bug.

_____

Here are two _____ my hats.

_____

Do _____ like hot dogs?

_____

I have _____ cats.

🍎 **Directions:** Write the missing word to finish each sentence. Color the pictures.

School + Home **Home Activity:** Have your child use the high-frequency words in other sentences.

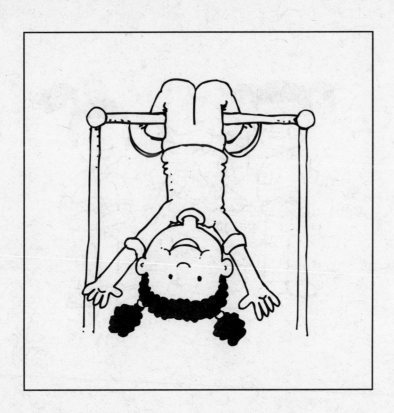

I am Jen.

I can hang from my legs.

What can you do?

4

What Can You Do?

Here is Ned.

Ned can run fast.

Ned can run and run.

1

Look at Ken.

He fed the big dog.

He fed the little dogs.

See Kim jump.

She can go from me to you.

She can jump from here
to here.

Name _____

 # Circle

 Directions: Look at the animal home. Which animal would live in this home? Circle the animal.

School + Home **Home Activity:** Have your child explain how he or she arrived at his or her conclusion.

Name _____

 Write

_____

- - - - - - - - - - - - - - -

_____

_____

- - - - - - - - - - - - - - -

_____

Directions: Write the word for each picture name.

School + Home **Home Activity:** Have your child write *mop* and *map* and draw a picture for each word.

Practice Book Unit 6

Name _____

 Circle  Color

She is _____.

mad

sad

glad

He is _____.

mad

sad

glad

 Directions: Circle the word to finish the sentence that tells how the person would feel. Color the pictures.

 Home Activity: Have your child tell why he or she drew the conclusion he or she did.

Practice Book Unit 6

Comprehension Draw Conclusions **59**

© Pearson Education K

Name _____

 Draw

The big dog

was on the bed.

One doll

had a little pup.

The man

sat in the mud.

A little pig

sat in the den.

 Directions: Draw lines to make complete sentences.

 Home Activity: Ask your child to make a new sentence using the sentence parts on the page.

Practice Book Unit 6